YOU NEVER BROKE MY HEART

Short stories by CW Evans

This book is dedicated to those who inspired it, whether or not they deserve it

LOVE NEVER WANTED ME

Indescribable pain. She lay on the bed, spread-eagled, eyes bulging out their sockets, her brain pounding. She could have been dead had it not been for the explosions in all of her nerve endings; huge roaring fiery and destructive.

She curled up onto her side and thought of the night before. She had made a fool of herself. The shameful images began to float in front of her, and the pain was no longer just physical, but a deep rooted ache deep within the canals of her brain. Shame burned like hot spikes gripped around her dignity. Dignity. What a joke. She had thrown it all away with every drink.

The many blackouts that dotted her memory probably hid the worst from her, but knowing the worst was there, that it existed in the first place, that was awful enough. It made her cringe inside. Made her curl her toes which lay hidden beneath the spiral of sheets she had kicked off during the morning.

I am a fucking mess.

There was no point getting up, or moving. She knew how the day would pan out. She would shake and shiver, possibly vomit, and her body would rage until late in the night. She would get hungry, and eat everything and anything. And she would not stop thinking about the night before. His face. An alcohol blur between them, a haze fitted across the memory, but she could still see it so clearly in one part, that one horrific moment, when he turned her down, rejected her, shook his head. But that one snatch, the tiny sliver, it wasn't enough. It would build bigger and bigger in her mind until she imagined the worst. But perhaps the worst wasn't what happened. But she would have no idea, because the memory was gone, it had gone down into the black with the last drink.

What was the last drink? She didn't remember. She thought of her empty purse. The money thrown away. Another stab of mental pain. Why did she lack the capability to stop? Why was it the drunker she got the more she wanted to get drunk? There was no line. And even if there was she wouldn't have any hesitation of crossing it, waving goodbye to it as it soared off into the distance behind her, as her limbs became harder to control, as her speech swirled from her lips and things were said that she never meant to say, or think, or ever create inside of her head.

She didn't want to see anybody for a long time. She closed her eyes and as her body temperature rose and fell like a sickening tide, she grasped tiny fragments of sleep and viewed the most grotesque of flashbacks, over and over, and disgrace painted every single scene.

Her body repaired itself over the following few days, but the pain inside of heart remained. A melancholy settled inside of her, as if she had been lined with a black snow. She found it difficult to leave the house; she shied away from social events. And she had no idea why. She must have known that nothing could have happened with him. He was married. The signs he had given, they hadn't been there, she knew that. She had grasped onto it all with false hope. She had built the connections out of her own delusional glass and it served her right that it had all fallen down on her head. She deserved nothing less than the shower of glass that was raining down on her now. She had been stupid and foolish and had behaved like a child. Adult relationships were much more complicated, much more bizarre. People said things; of course people said *things*, that's what people did. They express their inner desires, but nobody ever acts on them. But she had acted on hers. Had expressed them and acted upon them like a psychotic. She would cringe her entire body each time she thought of that night, which felt like every second of every day which followed.

It was like a trickling river of misfortune. She would meet somebody, some guy she thought was really fantastic, and she would think that he thought she was great too. But then it turned out he just wanted to be friends, or he'd stop talking to her altogether. Not one of her past fucks still spoke to her. Not of their own will anyway. The ones who were still pleasant would give her a courteous hello and a catch up if she reached out to them first. But not one of them wanted her again. Nobody wanted her, this she was sure of.

Her first and only real relationship, if she could even call it that, lasted barely six months. He had been younger than her, fit, attractive, with possibly an addiction to weed that surpassed her own addiction to alcohol. What began as a physical attraction, pure sex, spiralled into darkened evenings in smoke filled rooms, with bottles of cheap cider by the bed, the dense smell of cannabis soaked heavily into everything. She could feel herself becoming trapped, like an animal caught by the leg, and instead of trying to gnaw her way out, she lay back and took the pain. And then one day he was gone. What should have been a major relief felt like a major dent to her psyche. There had been nothing good about it, but she still felt as though she'd been washed up cold and alone, abandoned in some bizarre wasteland, left to find her own way out of a land she had been led into blind. And nobody felt her pain. Everybody told her how better off she was that he had finally unlatched his claws from her, but she couldn't shake off the feeling that if he didn't want her, the deadbeat youth with no prospects, no aspirations and no manners, then who would? And she had been right. Since then it had been disappointment after endless disappointment.

Another night and another disaster. She had been coaxed out by friends and because she was certain that she wouldn't see him, or any mutual friends, she had decided to take the plunge. The lure of a drink was too much for her, and the prospect of another two bottles of white wine in her tiny flat alone was just too much of a tragic comedy to bear. She had dressed up. First they went to a bar and the atmosphere felt comforting, and the cold wine in her hand like an old friend. When it was time to move on, she could hear the tiny voice in her ear, the one she always ignored, telling her to go home, to bid everyone goodnight and have a blissful white wine dream in her warm bed. But she couldn't do it. She went on to the club, where shots were handed to her, cheap rum and coke, a pitcher of strawberry daiquiri. She threw up. She didn't even make it to the toilet. She was stood by the bar and without warning the vomit flew up her throat and she tried to catch it, and without thinking rubbed it into her dress. And then the next thing she knew she woke up in her bed, naked, another hangover wracking her body as though she had spent the night on a bed of nails.

When she was younger she had often found herself on the outskirts of people. In school she had never belonged to one particular group of friends, but had simply moved among a few. At the time she had felt lonely and lost, desperate for a concrete footing amongst just a few people who enjoyed being her friend, who needed her as much as she needed them, instead of tolerated her. As she got older she realized that having one set of friends, who were all mutual, was an often rare and tiresome pursuit. She found that she coped better when she had different people to depend upon, who didn't know each other, and who couldn't turn the dynamic against her. The only downfall of these kinds of friendships was that people could drop out of the stratosphere for long periods of time, when she dropped from their minds for weeks or months at a time. They always resurfaced eventually, but the time in the wilderness could feel desperately lonely, and again she felt the familiar pang from her childhood, of being the one who had to be reached for, and never the one who could reach them.

In the morning she stood at her kitchen window drinking coffee. She was watching the birds in the hedge, their little heads popping in and out of the leaves, their tiny sporadic movements hypnotizing. In her drunkest moments, when she wasn't crippled by the self-conscious grip along her whole body and she could dance, she could feel like a bird, a tiny creature airborne and without restriction. She would close her eyes and skim the water of the seas, her feathery reflection shattered by the ripples of the pure speed that fell from her. Nobody could hold onto her, or trap her. She would land anywhere she wanted to, join any flock, fly to Africa, to the moon. Sometimes she didn't want anything else.

Sometimes she wanted children. She would awake early, before six, dawn just beginning, white sky and the sun piercing a burning hole in the horizon, and she would strain her ears into the silence of her empty flat, and she imagined she could hear her children. Babbling infants in the cot in the next room. The squeal of a baby on the monitor. Mommy! Mommy! Mommy! And her hands would slide down between her legs, and she'd feel herself, work two fingers up inside of her, feeling the dryness, the emptiness, the hollow of it all. And she couldn't imagine anything springing from such a depressing place. What kind of life could she give a child? All the love which was saturated inside of her, which had never been allowed out, sometimes she felt overcome by the need to give it to somebody, and she was just a bottle of wine away from running out into the night and fucking a random stranger without protection, hoping for the germination between them, so in nine months' time she could pour all that love onto a tiny human, a little boy or a little girl with squinty eyes and wrinkly little hands. But she knew it would all be false. It would be a different kind of love, a responsible love, not the wild fire that she'd start beneath her heart, which would billow smoke up and out of her stinging eyes like tears. Children would solve nothing but more problems, different kinds of problems.

When she was eighteen she had had an abortion. She had grown tired of holding onto her virginity. All her friends were in relationships. She was juggling university and trying to fit in, and no boy ever seemed to be interested in her. One night at the student union she had gone home with a boy – tall, blonde, a tight athletic body. He had mumbled a lot into her ear, and had driven inside of her his huge penis, which tore something in her and there was a lot of blood. She had crept out of the bathroom ashamed, but he was still there. "Never done a virgin before." He'd said, smiling. She got back into the warm bed and let him get on top of her again. This time it almost felt okay, but still so strange to have somebody that close. She felt almost vulnerable having another human being so deep inside of her. She felt relentlessly sick for a month and a half and the horror dawned on her that something was deeper still inside of her, and three pregnancy tests told her she was right. Driven by desperate fear she had gone through the usual channels, letting doctors talk down to her, letting nurses smile pitifully at her. And she had lay back on the bed and let them send her to sleep. When she awoke she felt instantly better. When she realized this she shrank back into shame and guilt. She felt better because she had had something ripped from her, something which had clung to her with tiny fingers, depended on her for life. Yet she hadn't thought twice about tearing it out. It was just an awful feeling. The guilt had grown back into the space where the baby had been. Thick and black and hideous. Leaving the clinic she fainted and was brought round by a nurse with watery grey eyes. She cried in the taxi on the way home and spent the week drinking and sleeping with more men.

She awoke one morning cold. She scrabbled around for her duvet, trying to pull its warmth up and around her, without opening her eyes which were threatening to explode. Her hands grazed cold wood. The feeling began to come back through her legs, her feet, she could feel that she was still wearing her tights. She squinted. The flood of the light hit her smack in the back of her retina. The pain was a searing firework straight into her brain. Where was she? She turned. The hardness of the surface beneath her bore into the softness of her skin, into the bones of her back. She shivered violently. She was wearing only her bra and her tights. She could see her shoes lying in a heap by the front door. She was somewhere between the door and the kitchen. Her hands over her face she sighed. Parts of the night began to come back, all hitting her with outstretched palms of embarrassment. She sat up onto her elbows. Everything was rocking now. A horrible sharp pain was running from the back of her head, the top of her neck, down over her shoulder. Her face felt numb along one side. Drool and spit had plastered her hair to her cheek. There was something wrong with her throat. The roof of her mouth had grown in size and was dry as dirt. Her face felt like it had suddenly shifted overnight, the bones clicking and snapping and reassembling over her skull, and the skin hadn't moved an inch.

Mascara had stuck her lashes to her face, so they stuck when she blinked, a sharp pain whenever she opened and closed her eyes.

There was somebody at the door. A big dark blue shape appeared at the frosted glass, and the letterbox opened with a deafening roar. White and brown shapes fell down on to the floor just a few feet away from her. She rose to her feet, shaking, not feeling real or grounded. The darkness of her bedroom welcomed her like the comforting arms of a lover. How something so intangible could be so soothing, so delicate around her, she felt like she was falling into a magical pool, a slave that was taking every pain out of her tortured body. But as she lay down on the bed, face first into the feather pillows, she could feel the old familiar nag, beginning as flood of nausea through the pit of her stomach, and it churned and created a current, which seeped into her nervous system. It made its way back up into her neck, into the backs of her eyes, into the core of her head, where it thundered and shook for the rest of the day.

Her image of a lover had not changed over the years. She thought it had. She thought she was getting more and more realistic. But the more real she thought of him, the beautiful lover who would appear one day and who would bring her the love she so badly wanted, when she created him from real men that she met or saw, the less shine he seemed to have. These imaginary relationships with these real life men would begin well in her head, she'd think it was almost possible – he wasn't perfect, so she had a chance, and she would look past his flaws and he would look past hers and things would be wonderful. But the more she thought about these real men, the more she could imagine the end. She saw the break-ups vividly in her mind. She heard their words, or hers, if in the rare instance she allowed herself to be the one breaking up with them. She even imagined their reconciliation, getting back together, smoothing over the cracks and trying to make it work. But it never did. It was always the same. She could imagine the all too real problems they would face, the prospects of fighting against something inevitable was too much of a wedge between reality and fantasy.

She always found herself returning back to the original lover, her dream lover. The one who was faceless but had the most beautiful face. The strong man who cut straight through to her core, who made the strings behind her ribcage twinge and sing. He would kiss the lids of her eyes. The palms of her hands. He'd smooth his fingers across her shoulders and down over her body. His face would be just millimetres away from hers. His breath soft like a ghost, hot and gentle across her nose, tickling the top of her lip. Sometimes she'd lie in bed and think about this lover, and she'd imagine him on top of her, and just the idea of his weight, the pressure on all the right places all over her body…she could come wildly to this fantasy, curling her toes under the covers, gripping onto the pillow beside her head, the waves of ecstasy crashing up and over her. She'd lie breathless, and he would retreat, always he would retreat, and she knew he'd never stay. He always left because he wasn't real. And the real ones always left because they were too real.

She had met him through friends. He was instantly friendly and was possibly the most beautiful man she had ever seen. When he spoke to her he would always look her directly in the eyes, and he'd laugh every time she said something sarcastic or dry. He'd sit close to her in the bar, or at whoever's house they were at. Their thighs would be grazing and she would feel the tingle all up that side of her body. She wanted to leap on him. Melt into him. She wanted his hands all over her, every inch of his skin touching every inch of hers. She wanted to be in his eyes, in his mouth, every part of her wet and delirious with happiness. But he was married.

One evening she had met friends at a bar in town. With her white wine in her hand she was speaking to a schoolteacher friend of hers, and she spotted him coming into the bar. He hugged everybody, and made his way over to where she was standing. He greeted her and smiled and she smiled back, and their mutual friend hugged him. Then a blonde woman seemed to enter the picture. She was short, pretty, with huge blue eyes. She shook her hand.

"This is my wife, Eleanor." He said.

She felt as though the floor had dropped from beneath her. What had everything been for? The electricity? The flirting? She felt brutally betrayed and as the bruises blossomed across her, black and ugly and there for the world to see, she went into hiding, petrified that he would sense something, would see the bruises he had just made, and then he would know what she had been thinking. He'd see her for the desperate fool she really was. She shrunk back from him, and from Eleanor, the beauty, the bitch.

She didn't see him for weeks. She dreamt about him twice. She lay in bed and waited for him to come crawling out of the back of her eyes. She couldn't get him out of her mind. Somehow knowing he was married, was unattainable, made her obsession with him grow. He was like a fungus all over her.

There was a music festival later that summer, and she went along with some friends. Cider and sunglasses and denim jackets. Naturally he was there. He sprung out from one of the tents as she walked past and bought her a drink. Eleanor was nowhere to be seen and she didn't want to ask. As the night drew in, she found herself getting more and more drunk. They shared a cigarette as a folk band played the last set of the night and he asked her if she was single.

"Yes." She said. And then, regrettably, "but you're not."

He laughed.

"No I'm not." He said. "But you know, if I was going to cheat, I don't know, it would be with you. Maybe."

"Maybe? That's nice. Thanks a lot."
"Definitely."

"But you're not going to cheat."
"No I'm not."
"That wouldn't be nice."
"It really wouldn't."
"Only weak people cheat."
"Yeah?"
"Yeah."

And then he kissed her. It was strong and gentle at the same time. The caress of his lips on hers was so soft, as was the tongue that slid slowly in to touch hers. But the drive behind it, the passion, it felt like a storm was suddenly breaking, raging into her from somewhere deep inside of him.

They kissed for a long time. Then he wanted another beer so they went to hunt for one, and found everybody by the tents. He began to chat wildly and animatedly to everybody. Everybody but her. She began to yawn just as the sky was lightening, and realizing she was being well and truly ignored she crawled into her tent and passed out in her sleeping bag.

When she was a little girl, she had watched her parents split up, get back together, and split up again. Within months they both found other people. And she thought then it would all be okay because it looked like love was easy to find.

MODERN LIFE

Morning after

I throw myself out of bed. My head is exploding, my eyes bulging from their sockets, my cheeks filling up with white froth which spills out as I grip the edge of the toilet bowl. I shudder, horrific movements through my entire skeleton, joints cracking, tensing. My stomach lurches over and over and everything pours out of me, out of my mouth, and into the water below. Memories from last night flood the darkness behind my eyes. Flashbacks with the smell of cigarettes, the rancid taste of cheap wine, the image of the smiling beautiful boy I kept talking to, convinced we could end up in bed together. Shame replaces the blood in my veins and the rotting begins again, the decaying of my mind, my soul and the endless blackening of my heart. Failure rings like a brass bell inside, and I am thrown from curved wall to curved wall against the cold violent metal and as I heave again into the depth of the toilet, I wish with every screaming cell in my wracked body that I could turn back time, that I could go back to last night and not do half the things I did, not say half the things I said, and not drink half as much as I did.

Sober

I have an early morning at work so I don't drink. I turn off the lights early and lie in bed. But I can't sleep. I can't sleep sober. I wonder how many people do it. I lie on my side wide awake, eyes staring ahead in the dark, my brain grinding in motion, everything going through, processing, again and again, horrible images, this living nightmare. Memory, recollection, recapping the events of today, yesterday, last week. When my eyes grow heavy my whole body reacts; my legs feel stiff, the twinges of seizure awaken in the front of my skull, and I'm scared to close my eyes. Maybe there's something wrong with me, something I can't see. I turn over in the dark. The same process. I push the covers away from my body, and then pull them back up. The dark room stays dark and I know out there people are asleep, their blood free of toxic. But here I am, empty blooded and awake, staring at the crack of light from the streetlamp outside, spilling into my room, its yellow claw stretched across the wall and curving around the edge of the ceiling, and I feel tired just thinking about waking up in the morning.

Town

I walk through town and I feel the concrete burn my feet beneath me. I feel like a demon swimming in holy water. Everything around me is so offensive, so stagnant, so cruel to every inch of me that I react so horribly each time I tread the same streets, see the same buildings, the same tree, the same wisp of sea between the hotels on the curve of the hill. I don't want to be here anymore. I breathe the air in my garden and it's toxic, it scorches me from the inside out, it singes my eyelashes and scrapes the cells from my tongue. Like potassium in water I explode when I face the same shelves full of the same shit in the same shops, I vibrate away in invisible columns of purple and white amongst the commercial despair, the clothes with the tags still on, and all the shoes lying footless on the shelf, useless. I dream of the other places. The other concrete jungles with something new every day, vibrancy exploding from every window on every street; the beaches lying empty and soulless, free from the tan bodies and pot bellies and beer cans; the mountainous regions which spiral high into the ether, hidden by clouds at the top, always wet, sodden in sky tears, the endless snow cascading down on the very tips of the highest points of earth. The thick vegetation of the deepest jungles, coiling like an elaborate web, heavy vines twisting around dizzyingly high trees, blocking out the sun, and the night and the in between. I want to sit on the porch of a tiny town, three houses long with a rusty petrol garage. Endless sky over corn fields. Rain slick grey stones paving the way down to a stormy sea, surrounded by even greyer hills and black skies. Torrid heaths and dirt tracks, beaten paths down to ancient country houses. All this vomits from my mind into my eyes as I stare around this turgid little town. Everybody here lives or dies or gets away.

A SHOWER AT MIDNIGHT

He stares into the darkness. The stain in the sink. The mosaic reflection in the window. His face, broken up into tiny circles, flesh and blue and pink.

I'm an idiot...

He thinks there is nothing left now. Nobody left... just the black streak across old enamel, already layered with dust, speckled with time. And in his eyes he sees the cold whipped branches of the lifeless trees. The years that have swollen by and burst like waves rolling through the sea. The violent froth spreading out on the sands. As the final white bubbles ebb and burst away...

My body will never be anything but something that carries my mind. Just a brittle skeleton filled with pain and skin. And on top of it this crazy electric palace. My stupid brain!

The sight in the full length mirror, the spindly legs, the purple patches of skin spread out over bad circulation, the scattering of spots and thick, black, coarse hairs and the lines. This is not a body, this is a wreckage...

And this mind is a vortex of everything I've seen, every mistake I carelessly made, and chose to make, the knife across the canvas, warm hilt in my hand. The images and the gaps, the spaces in between, all the moments I breathed and saw but I don't remember. Like smoke vanishing out of the window.

But out the window lies the blackness, the never ending. The future. Sometimes we breathe and hold it in, and sometimes we think about never letting it out again.

If only our lungs could burst, like pink balloons, sharp and shocking. And taking us away in that frightening moment, loud and unnatural, but quickly and painlessly.

That's how I would like to go...

Goodbye to this body, he wants to say, taking the thin sliver of flesh between forefinger and thumb. If it was easy to pull the mind out through the nose as it is to elicit cum from a hard cock. The stimulate and excite until that glorious moment, pulsating and beautiful, explosions of white behind the eyes, and then the mind shoots out at 30 miles per hour. Out into the open. Into the nothing...

Spirals and spirals.

I am in the night now. And try as you might, nobody can lift the sun.

SLEEPING WITH YOU

I want to die. Everything unfair and hideous boils up inside my stomach like pure black rot and I stare at you with him, with them.

So much beauty, so much hate.

Naked skin on skin I'm twisted with this want, lying wide awake, sleeping with you. When I close my eyes I'm transported to you. When I open them I'm here again.

Four AM and we're all sat outside in the rain, drunken babbling, you're kissing him and I try not to look, the fear behind my eyes; instead I focus my eyes on the distant dawn, the shining wet roads, the drizzle in front of the streetlamps.

I never wanted to love you.

I hear your laughter and it rings like knives in my ears, this pain in the side of my head, this drunken despair in the pit of my stomach, the soles of my feet, this sting on my body where your fingers have been. The pulse in my throat quickens under the skin you used to bite and I feel the ghosts of your kisses and your tongue across the backs of my legs, under my knees, watery lines through my middle.

Maybe it's time to go home.

He finally leaves and your selfishness pours all over me like bricks, I'm coughing dust, bones snapping as I hurtle to the floor under the weight of it all.

You're a sick sick fuck you're so cruel and I'm just as pathetic.

My crooked puppy body limps back like always and tonight I'm sleeping with you again, lying next to you, the morning rolling in with the swathes of grey clouds and the heavy rain continues lights up all of my bruises and blows and you sleep and you sleep on and on and on and not one word from you not any acknowledgment and maybe now I know the price of it all.

I sold my soul for your body on mine and I never knew it could be as empty as this.

STANLEY & ERIC – A LOVE STORY

I was fifteen when I first met Stanley and Eric. I had been drinking in the park with friends all night and was vomiting gloriously into a bin when they walked past me, hand in hand, and stopped to ask if I was alright. Between spitting up globs of rainbow puke I told them I was fine thank you and waved them on, but they stayed and Stanley rubbed my back whilst Eric told me that he still ended up in this state despite being twenty years old. When I was able to stand up straight and my stomach wasn't spinning, I thanked them again and they hugged me and walked off into the night.

When I was eighteen and old enough to stop drinking in parks, I met Stanley and Eric again. I recognized them instantly – Stanley, tall and brunette with an orange face; Eric, a bit shorter and paler, a bit pudgy, with bleached blonde hair. They didn't recognize me but I stood in the corner of the dance floor staring at them for a long time. I had kissed some boys, pretty ones with black hair and thin noses. I had cried over much of the same boys, their attitudes and fleeting disappearances confused me. But there was something about Stanley and Eric. Something in their eyes and the way they looked at each other, that drew me towards me. I could feel a magnet in my stomach. I wanted to know them. I wanted to crawl into their world and be comfortable between them.

Sergio sidled up next to me, his hard chest pushing against mine, his fingers brushing my waist.

"Who have you seen?" He hissed into my ear. I didn't say anything; I just looked into his brown eyes and let him kiss me. I shrugged. My eyes stayed on Stanley and Eric, who were at the bar, talking to a big crowd of people. Sergio's hand touched my cock and it was hard and he got the wrong idea and grinned at me. I shook my head. I wasn't going home with Sergio. I couldn't stomach his animal grunts and rough hands again. Eventually he took the hint and moved onto Jem, whose eyes were rolling in his head and I suspected he was on some pretty strong stuff as usual. When the group moved on I stayed behind. I didn't tell them, I just vanished into the toilets and ignored their calls and texts. I emerged when I was sure that they had gone and I glanced up towards the bar to make sure Stanley and Eric were still there, and they were, so I dug cash out of my pockets and walked towards them. I stood beside them at the bar as I waited to be served. I watched them out of the corner of my eye. Eric was staring intensely at the dance floor. His eyes studied the dancing bodies under the vivid lights with complete and utter concentration. I wondered if he was searching for somebody. Maybe somebody who broke his heart years ago, before he met Stanley.

I bought a drink and then stayed at the bar. I turned around and pressed my back against it. I saw a short guy I once kissed. He had a boyfriend now, who was even shorter than he was. They stared at me and I looked away and saw Stanley staring at me. He smiled, his teeth perfect white against his tanned face, and I smiled back, a slightly smaller smile because my teeth weren't as white as his. Eric's trance broke and he looked away from the dancers and looked at me, as if he shared a psychic connection with Stanley. Eric smiled too. He leaned in towards me.

"You live here?" He asked. I was surprised at how deep his voice was. I just nodded. "I'm Eric. This is Stanley." He pointed behind him at Stanley's head which leaned in now over Eric's shoulder. I told them my name and they told me they were pleased to meet me, and that they had spotted me around. A popular song came on and they both cheered and finished their drinks and then they grabbed me by an arm each and pulled me down onto the dance floor. The lights were pink and white and I was in the middle of a big crowd and we were all dancing. We bought more drinks and then I felt drunker than I wanted to be. Stanley and Eric looked as composed as ever and I told them and said that I admired them and they laughed and smiled and petted me like a puppy and then I was in a taxi with them, squeezed up against the door as they sat with their hands in each other's laps. I didn't ask where we were going but I wasn't surprised when we drove towards a posh area of town where the flats were all new and spacious and going fast.

As we went up in the lift I tried to make myself sober up. I stared at the mirror in the tiny space and I tried to force my pupils smaller, but the more effort I exerted the more my vision blurred. Stanley and Eric held hands and watched me. They laughed when I gasped at the size of their flat as we stepped inside. It was huge and pristine with a deep cream carpet and oak varnished frames around the photos that hung on the smooth white walls. The lights flickered on in the kitchen and nothing was out of place. I stood unsteadily on the black and white chequered tiles and Eric handed me a glass of Pepsi. The bubbles popped under my nose as I drunk the sweet liquid. I drained the glass and felt the sugar work. I wanted to be sober for whatever was going to happen next.

Somebody had different plans however. As we walked into the living room I began to feel worse, and I felt myself lose my grip on my own body. I felt lighter and lighter until all I could feel was the top of my head; I was hanging to myself by my own eyeballs. The rest of me was drifting above like smoke. Everything swam around me. I sat on the leather couch and it was warm and soft and I felt scared. I wanted the leather to be cool and slippery. I wanted it to feel like leather. I felt skin next, as Stanley took my hands, linking his fingers with mine, and then his lips pressed against my mouth and I felt the hot eel of his tongue poke through my teeth.

"Relax." He whispered, sounding like he'd said it three times. I tried to. But the more I tried to pull myself down from the air back into my skin, the more I could feel myself tensing up. I swore I heard all my muscles creaking, the sinew whining with the strain, the bones clicking as they fixed rigid in my frame.

"Just relax…" Eric was more forceful. He stood on the other side of the coffee table, something in his hands, which he was staring at.

Stanley tried to kiss me again, and this time it was more successful. He kissed harder and harder, and then I felt his hands on my cock and I couldn't tell if I was hard or not.

Suddenly I was on the floor, the ceiling above me slipping past like a conveyor belt, winding to the left and then back to the right. A chill rippled through me and I felt fabric being torn from my body. I was naked. A dark shape lowered itself towards my eyes, and I smelt the familiar odour of cock and balls and ass. Instinctively I stuck out my tongue and flicked it against the warm tight flesh of Stanley's asshole. I raised my hands and gripped his thighs, pulling him down tighter onto me.

"That's it." Eric's voice crooned from above. "That's nice."

I had no idea who was above me now, but I kept licking and kissing and sucking in tiny pouts against the warm skin, and then a cock was slipped in between my teeth and I opened my jaw wide in panic. I began to suck slowly, feeling the textured surface of the shaft rub against my lips, and then it began to push further and further in. All my air seemed to be squeezed out of me, and I inhaled through my nose in huge gulps, the smell of sweat and ass filling me in huge pungent clouds. The cock went further and further in until it was jabbing against the soft flesh at the back of my throat. I felt myself gag and I inhaled more of the spicy, overpowering air, and then I tried to push whoever it was off of me but they didn't move at all and instead just pushed down further.

"That's it, take it, take it…" Eric sounded so far away I thought I had actually gotten lost inside the body and soul that was pushed down on top of me. My eyes rolled back. I stopped taking in the air. It was useless. I let my jaw go slack and felt my mouth close slightly. The cock rubbed against my lower teeth and then slowed down, and pulled out slightly. Little morsels of air crept in around it and it was so cool against the inflamed redness of my throat that I sucked it in as greedily as I could. As Stanley – or Eric – got off of me completely I felt a hiccup well up from my chest and I burped. The burp became bubbles and I was a second late in recognizing the familiar warning. I felt the vomit gurgle up my throat and up into the back of my nose and it rushed into all the passages inside my head and it was hot and stinking and I tried to cough to push it out but it just brought up more and then I began to actually cough and choke and I tried to breathe through it all and it was thick over my tongue, tasting of mushrooms and bad wine. I shut my eyes and felt somebody grab my shoulders and then I rode into the darkness on a tidal wave of hot yellow blood.

THE MOST BEAUTIFUL MAN IN THE WORLD

In black satin sheets I fantasized about this guy, lying on top of me, his slender frame bones in soft skin lying on top of mine, his lips pressed against my neck.

When I look at him my heart bursts overfilled with need and want and admiration and lust and plain fucking desperation.

He stands, almost six foot, in his black shirt and his spiky cheek bones and he speaks with a drudging tone like all his words swim in treacle before escaping his perfect mouth, his straight teeth and his beautiful cockeyed smile.

He laughs, a trill like a wave crashing on my forehead, his steps as he walks beyond me like the stabbing of a horse's hooves in the soft crush of the surf under grey sky, my mother's favourite painting.

I lie on the hard floor and imagine him walking across me, his weight stamping on all of my organs forming beneath him, his beautiful bare feet pushing into my mouth, his rare flesh like molluscs on my puckering skin my screaming skin.

We danced one night in a church, everybody was drinking and I was spiralled in hell, surrounded by these people in cropped tees and tiny dresses and plastic hair and our amorous bridges grew and he kissed me in the confusion of drunken want.

A monkey in a leather jacket. A circus freak in the circle of normality, under the balcony of entitled gaze.

Maybe I was shackled. Maybe he was just drunk.

Sometimes I dream of his blood dripping into my mouth as he tightens the belt and I shudder and the fissure burns the tender root of my tongue and into the darkness of myself he cascades and fades into my acid that destroys all and everything.

Like a dead tree my fingers scrape this living earth. The bloom of his potential.

I am nothing to his everything.

PLEASE DO NOT REJECT ME

First one, his come hit my tongue like a barrage of lemons and salt, an onslaught of tequila and burnt matches, vile and sizzling, and I spat it out immediately, across his stomach.

Second one, came in his pants within minutes as he rubbed up against me.

"Hold on." He said, as he climbed up between my legs. I touched him and felt the sticky wet spot on the fabric of his underwear.

He pumped out four more the rest of the night.

The third never came at all. I sucked at his drunk flaccid cock in the darkness, fell asleep and heard him leave in the morning and he never spoke to me again.

Fourth and fifth blended into one, young and awkward bodies, their come invisible in the dark, just the cold touch as I grazed my elbow across their stomach a little later on.

Six straddled my chest and came into my mouth.

I closed my eyes and turned my head and felt the hot spray hit my top lip, my chin, my eye and the back of the my throat.

A salty hot bitterness. Easier this time.

Eight lay in the darkness and took ages.

My arm grew tired and I was drunk and I wanted to go to sleep. Eventually I felt his body spasm beneath my cramping hand. He wiped his shoulder and let me roll over and submit to my hangover.

Nine wanted me to come first but his technique was rough and mechanical. I shrank in his touch and he kept pulling away from me, warning me he was going to come.

Eventually I grew bored and grabbed him until he came across my hand reluctantly.

Ten pushed my face into the inflatable mattress I was using as a bed at the time and ignored my repulsion and shrivelling of my skin and body and when the moment arrived he climbed up on my chest and shoved his dick into my mouth, into the back of my throat, and I had no choice but to swallow the lot.

I threw up afterwards.

Eleven let me suck his tiny cock while we watched awful films and he would announce that he was going to come before shooting a thin stream of white across his stomach.

I wiped it up with toilet roll and sat next to him as he refused to touch me again and the film finished.

Twelve was the complete opposite, a beast that I couldn't get my whole hand around, and he kissed me constantly, and when he came I felt his balls shrink up suddenly, his scrotum tightening and hardening like walnut shells.

Thirteen shot violently up my back as I straddled him.

Fourteen held me at his side as he came and I felt it hit behind my ear, into my hair.

Fifteen lay below me, my feet straddled across his stomach, under his cock, his breath loud in my crotch.

Sixteen let me kiss him all over, pleaded with me to lick his balls as he came across his stomach.

Seventeen asked me to finger him as he came, asked me to swallow, I kissed the hot wet tip but let nothing pass my lips.

Even the ugliest among us have made our lovers beg.

WHITE

I was in the sun and I didn't understand why. Just a few hours ago I was in a dark club and I was drinking, the only lights coming from the strobes and the lasers and the neon which outlined everything.

Now the natural light hurt my eyes and was burning my nose and my neck. Somehow I had ended up at an after party on a rooftop. I could see the sea from here under the pale blue sky, under the white hot sun. The blood in my veins bubbled and boiled in the heat and I found shade by the wall near a trellis. The flowers were dead, parched in the heat, the hostess swaying in a summer dress, everybody else lying down in the middle, not burning, not melting, their perfect bodies only getting browner and tighter. And I was getting weaker and weaker.

Inside the house there was no escape from the sun. It streamed through every window, so many windows, and it lit up the dust in the air, sapped everything of its colour.

I turned on the tap and drunk water from the kitchen. Somebody passed me a can of beer. I popped it open and felt the cold froth hit my hands and for a second I knew what comfort felt like.

I could smell baby oil and suntan lotion and cigarettes. I opened my mouth and said things I instantly regretted.

Out on the roof most people had paired off. Two boys lay on their stomachs, their arms around one another's shoulders; they looked like they were flying – the sky would take them anywhere and everywhere and I felt the concrete firm under my own feet.

I stayed in the sun as long as I could, just to belong, just to be amongst the group, to hear their chatter, to listen to their voices singing things about their lives and things I had always wanted to know. Here I had penetrated the shell. I was in the pressure cooker amongst the subjects I had so viewed like a voyeur for so long. But it was too hot. I was becoming a husk, uglier than usual amongst the beautiful faces, and my youth didn't matter.

Inside the house again, by the bathroom, somebody held a baggie of cocaine in my direction. I said no, I did not want any, but before it was swung away from me towards somebody else I noticed that it was the most brilliant white I had ever seen.

THANK YOU DREW, WHEREVER YOU ARE

Autumn evening, a lazy orange sky, hanging low above the horizon, above the smudged black outlines of the trees; I'm standing on the porch, watching the sun set, aware I'll never catch the final moment as it vanishes beneath the edge of the earth, but I am enjoying the deathly rich colours that make me want to cry. It's been a laborious day. Digging earth up from the roots of the trees out on the east, in harsh sun and heat, my tiny straw hat doing nothing to protect me from the beating rays on my back, cooking me. The orange earth piled up like a fresh grave. I looked it and I thought of you.

Your mother's funeral. Bang in the middle of our gripping friendship, our feverous love as they came to call it. A hot summer's Sunday at the graveyard, us sweating in black, the open grave, a maw ready to swallow your first love. The woman who had given birth to you, ravaged hopeless by cancers and by life. Her eyes closed forever in the shined oak box, lowered into the ground, into the darkness. I held your hand when I was sure they weren't looking, and felt my own body drip beneath my collar with sweat and tears. It was an awful day.

The cry of some unseen bird out in the wiry bush, the call of wildlife going around their day by day, following their natural instinct. I walk down the porch steps and onto the driveway and I go up to the gate. I'm aware that I can't go any further, and I stare out into the land, dried and sparse, dotted with the husks of the trees that survive out here and the bush, the invincible vegetation that doesn't care about shade or water, it lives on and on and on. The hot wood of the gate under my hand reminds me of the shovel in my hand earlier today. The grip of my livelihood. The bark of the trees from our youth.

At night we would run out into the woods beyond our suburban nightmare, and we would down cans of cheap beer and kiss feverishly behind the black oaks and climb up onto the branches and sit nestled in the arms of the giants and you'd hold me and then I'd hold you and if it ever got cold we'd push ourselves together and heat ourselves up with our breaths. The smell of your hair was like olives and soap. The prickle of your unshaved chin like a scourer against the back of my neck.

One early morning you nudged me awake and I squinted up at the dawn piercing through the tops of trees and the shimmer of the new day made me shiver and I rubbed my eyes and sat up. We were surrounded by light. I stared at you until I couldn't get used to the beauty and I glared at the soil beneath my palms. You rubbed my back and I shrugged closer and closer to your body until you wrapped me in your arms and you whispered "Let's go." And we walked for what felt like miles until we got home and we both made our excuses, so different yet strikingly the same and nobody questioned us. In your pool a few days later somebody pulled my leg and dragged me under the water and I fought against the blue and the white bubbles that frothed in rage from my screaming mouth until I was allowed to surface and he laughed and called me a faggot and told me he knew what was going on. I was shaken, and I climbed out and got changed. You asked what was wrong and I told you I thought things were changing. You pressed me for more but I felt that I couldn't give any more and I went home.

I step back into the house and I close the door on the orange haven outside. The darkness yawns all around me, welcomes me back into its crevices, and I head into the dining room. The large table, cleaned and emptied since dinner, is mine. The silver candlesticks are mine too. The polished oak cabinet decorated in silver is also mine. Everything here belongs to me. Everything worked for and earned. Each dollar sweated and bled from my pore throughout the years. It goes dark outside and I close the curtains. The TV turns on in the other room, and I go out back into the hall and upstairs. I open the closet in the bedroom and stare at the rows of shirts against the brown wood background, streaked black for effect. I touch the cotton and there is one shirt which, almost, reminds me of the day we caught the train into the city. It's a white and faded pink colour; it looks like long ago it could have been red.

You were so proud of it, your red and white checked shirt. You wore it with your black jeans and told me you looked like a rock star. I couldn't take my eyes off you, and you put on sunglasses and we caught the morning train into the city and I sat near the door and you stood, leaning against the buttons, and people kept making you move and you shrugged and then kept going back there to stand. When we got to the city we went straight down the smallest road we found. We walked endlessly down dead ends and road blocks and eventually we ended up in the big streets and we bought lunch and ate at a bus stop. We watched the people come and wait and get onto the buses as they pulled up every other minute, their doors hissing and squealing as they opened, tortured by the endless routine, the tires groaning in our minds as they veered off back into the traffic and onto their journeys. We browsed second hand stores and I stared at discarded things whilst you stroked my back and you bought me a harmonica that was engraved with a hummingbird and I used my shoelace to tie it around my neck and near the fountain, as the evening was settling in, an old couple asked to take our picture. You grabbed my shoulders and we smiled for the camera and the old man asked if we were students and we shook our heads and laughed and the old woman told us we were handsome young men and in her eyes I could see that she didn't, and would never, have any grandchildren.

We got home late that night and I faced the wrath of my parents and I was told I wasn't allowed to see you ever again but they were using that old threat more and more and it just wouldn't stick. I waited three days before going round to your house. You answered the door in a faded blue shirt and told me you couldn't go anywhere. You had a bruise around your eye. We went up to your room and played chess but not really concentrating and when your dad's car pulled up in the driveway your eyes widened slightly and the front door opened and slammed shut and you asked me to leave. I knew what was going on. I left and as I turned at the bottom of your driveway you were stood in your bedroom window and you waved and I blew you a kiss and you laughed.

I sit in the bath, letting it soak up the day's work, the sweat and the red dust and the dirt. My feet prod the dripping taps at one end and I lie with my neck draped over the other. The water goes cold around me. My wife knocks on the bathroom door and asks how much longer I'm going to be. I don't know. I don't know how much longer I'm going to be. But I pull out the bathplug all the same and water gurgles down the drain. In bed my wife reads with the bedside lamp on and I turn onto my side away from her. My eyes are heavy.

You moved away unexpectedly one summer. I got a letter from you, your looping signature at the bottom and three kisses. I wrote you back and the letters kept up a steady pace, but they got shorter, and then the weeks between them became longer. I moved away for an apprenticeship, and in the winter when I returned another letter was waiting for me on my freshly made bed. I tore open the envelope and read it and smiled and wrote a reply. I kept catching glimpses of that return letter throughout the holidays, always meaning to post it, and on my last day before I left to go back to my apprenticeship it was left on the table by the front door so I wouldn't forget. But I did forget.

Another morning comes with the buzz of the alarm clock. The rise of the sun in the yellow sky brings another flurry of unearthed soil and the acrid smell of hydraulic lubricant and the hum of the diggers. And another day of searching the distance for you, Drew, my love. The knot of regret still there over that last unsent letter, and the years in between now and then. Maybe it was cowardice that made me forget to send it. You were always the brave one. Did you remain brave? Was that the kind of man you grew to become? In the prism of the past the paths are there. All the paths I took and the paths you might have taken, and between them, the paths we didn't take. I don't even have that harmonica anymore. But thank you Drew, wherever you are.

DOG

I miss my dog.

Almost four am sitting alone in the dark just the light from the TV, watching nothing, drinking cider, feeling like my life is drying up now that my youth has fled, turning brown like leaves and dropping away, and I turn and his face would be there, looking up, wide eyed and innocent.

The best person I had ever met in my life.

Four legs, big brown eyes, a panting tongue over the yellowish ridges of teeth drool spilling hot slimy wet. Pure love.

Human touch under his chin, eyes closed for a second, yes that's it, eyes open looking up looking sideways looking back up, never begging but always thirsty for attention.

Put my face next to his, the pink tongue loops out and licks my face in four quick movements, its warm wet against my chin, against my lips, the thick smell of dog food, of dog breath, his little paw reaching up trying to rest on the crook of my elbow, never quite staying there, giving up and setting down on my knee. Pure love.

I stumble home as the dawn cracks the black sky outside and lie spinning on my bed and the comfort of his body stretched out next to mine, the many fibers of his hair under my touch, the slow steady rise of his breathing lying there as I slip out of consciousness, and still there when I wake up seven hours later in the burning sunlight streaming through my window, and lost in the acidic sea of a hangover.

Vomiting and holding onto the sides of the toilet my knees on the cold tile floor, and he licks my bare back. Pure love.

Salt tears over another boy and his nuzzling cold wet nose approaches and closes in, and that curling tongue slicks out and licks them away.

Hidden away in my room the outside world all festering from my shame, absolute hatred down the telephone lines, I can't take my words back and bridges have been burnt, but he eats the food I lay out for him and curls up over my stomach and never judges me not once, even when he rolls onto his back for me to scratch his stomach as I walk past, but instead I walk over him and don't stop.

I scratch him later feeling wretched, but he doesn't bring it up, doesn't chastise, and I never shrink or curl up or die because of anything he says or does.

Now I don't feel heavy enough, now his weight is missing from my frame and my hands yearn for the smooth roughness of his coat and his smell and most of all his unconditional never ending never changing never faltering and never shrinking love.

My dog.

NOW WHAT

Sprawled out on the floor amongst the papers and the magazines and the spilled tobacco, my shape like a corpse, I glare at the hardwood floor, blinking.

Somewhere in the room somebody else is scrabbling about, I hear the clink of glasses, the sound of something rolling across the table and falling off with a thump.

The light changes as morning comes.

I stay where I am, face down, waiting for something to change. My eyes grow tired but I force them open, staying awake and staring at the floor, staring at the grooves in the wood, the particles of dust, the remnants of me.

Maybe I have died.

Maybe you had finally grown tired of all my shit and struck out at me, hitting me across the head with the first blunt thing you got your hands on, probably one of your many ashtrays, and my scalp would split and my skull would crack, break inwards, and I'd fall into this position where I am now, and die of trauma to the brain.

But I can hear my shallow breathing.

I can feel its warmth as it pushes back off the floor and back into my face. I can feel the beads of moisture on my upper lip as it condenses there on my cold skin.

I think about everything I've done for you:

Getting up to meet you in the middle of night after you wake me up halfway through sweating out a fever so I'm ill for another day; waited long hours in my darkened room alone and drinking staring mindlessly at the television; let you bite me on the neck, giving me big dark bruises that last for days; pretended that I didn't care for you; pretended that I didn't want you around.

I pretended that I didn't love you.

I think about moving, about propelling my body up like a sack of meat and let my blood move in my veins, but my limbs lie here weighed down by my own apathy.

I don't want to move ever again.

Somebody comes into the room once more, I hear their feet shuffling, I feel the vibrations in the wood against my face.

"Get up." I don't. "Get up now."

I stretch my arms out in front of me, my knuckles scrape the wooden leg of the sofa.

"I'm not getting up." I say.
"I'm not getting up, ever."
"Fine."

The squeal of the hinges as the door opens, and then the dull crack of wood against doorframe as you slam it shut.

Gone gone gone.

No different now than it's always been.

You've been gone for so long I don't remember a time when you were ever really here.

A HOLE IN MY HEART

No morning as bitter as one after you had been so kind to me the night before.

I had rested on your chest as we watched TV and you shifted to get comfortable and I moved away.

"Put your head back there" you said.

The darkness of your room and the shadows created from the artificial blur of the television were sucked out of the window by morning, as the grey dawn arrived and stirred me from my fitful sleep against your hot body with its chilling lick across my bare shoulders.

The stench of cannabis filled the tiny room and permeated my hair and flesh and the soft membrane inside of me, your bedcovers were stiff with come and spilt beer and thick with the scent of you and I wrapped it around my body as I pulled myself from you and you lay still, snoring softly, your hair skimming across your closed eyes, your chest rising in rhythm with the noise, your warm feet nestled on mine.

There was ash on the pillow between us, left from your last joint hours ago or from the passion between us I couldn't tell.

I rubbed it between my fingers, the grey smudges across my skin like dead hickeys, all the love sucked out, leeched with a vampire's enthusiasm leaving nothing but white parched shells reaching out from the palm of my hand.

I wish you had sucked the life out of me.

I couldn't sleep again, not like you, sleeping solidly for hours filled with smoke and booze, I was rattling empty on vodka with a churning stomach and every time I closed my eyes I saw you heavy above me, grinding your crotch into mine, your sweat dashed chest touching mine, and my legs wrapped around your hips, and I grew achingly horny, but I was too weak and sick to reach out for you.

I tossed and turned, hoping to wake you up, to startle you into a sleepy embrace, to have you press your body close up on me, but you stirred slightly and mumbled, and you turned your body over, away from me, giving me your back, dotted with the occasional mole or spot, no sign of my fingers which had gripped so feverishly earlier, holding on as if I wanted you to melt into me, to give me something via osmosis, something to make me feel better, to make this sick longing go away.

When I came across your stomach I felt as though I had gotten there, as if I had gotten that elusive something, but when the pulsing in my groin ebbed away it came flooding back into the pit of my stomach, and spread like ink in blotting paper, a darkness which ate away at my living core.

SUMMER

You bastard.

In the long grass in summer, twisted like valves of our own hearts, the halo of the sun in blinding rings, smashing into the back of my eyes, retinas burning with the globs of yellow light which fire up your silhouette before me, your hair backlit, an angel.

MY SKIN BURNING.

From the lazy heat and the shame, the iron shame rattling around my bones, solid grasp on my marrow, my atoms splitting, my cells dying with the raging humiliating fever.

FUCK YOU.

I slither with the cobra as it wraps itself around my body.

The venom I can smell, the venom thick and honey like, dripping from fangs so close to my face, and christ I can feel the humidity of the day seeping into my flesh like a sponge.

I fill up. I expand and I lie in the grass as you waver above me in the quivering air and you stare down at me and I die, I simply die, and let the earth eat my body and the worms slither through my eyes these useless vessels of bulbous flesh and nerves.

THE RAPID DECLINE OF FEELINGS WHICH EXIST ONLY IN THE CHEMICAL CANALS OF THE MIND AND WHICH CAN MAKE ALL THE DIFFERENCE TO THE OTHER PERSON

Can't close the curtain so the rain billows in, wet sheets hitting my face, my skin.

I blink rapidly, breaking up the night outside in tiny shutter clicks like a camera. Click, click, click.

I can feel you watching me, I can hear your breathing, laboured with a love that is now decayed by hate, or indifference, thick and cloying at the back of your throat.

Move on, to move on, and wish your demons away.

You ask me to turn, to look at your face one last time, but I refuse. I stand and get wetter, wetter still. The cold light of the moon on the city surface, a pale blanket smothering everyone asleep and awake.

I can smell the smog of the streets, I can smell your sweat as it trickled down the nape of your neck.

My ribs ache for the touch of your hands, your enveloping arms again around my chest and stomach, but I remain torturously empty like the vessel I am, I was born empty I live on empty and one day I will die empty, my hands void of any of your remaining cells.

No trace left on this parched, loose skin, the grooves in my palm empty rivers of dust, the only evidence that I have lived the deep death rattle of my last breath as it seeps out of my chest.

You tell me to take care.

Take care.

My whole world lies rancid in this tiny room, everything I own in dusty piles around my old bed.

It can take care of itself.

Take care of yourself you say.

I pull the curtain as hard as I can and the hooks on the rail break and snap off like teeth bullied out of a bloody mouth, they click and patter as they hit the floor and the material of the drapes drops heavy in my hands.

The door closes. You've left. You've left me.

AND RIGHT THERE FOR A MINUTE, I KNEW YOU SO WELL

I dreamt about you last night, drunk under the bus stop lights.
Full of vodka and ego, you swilled around in your young body,
ravaged almost ancient by excesses, by the touch of all the old
men you sold your body to.

You'd flick your hair and laugh meanly at innocent things I'd say
to try and impress you. You hung around me despite your never
ending degrees of criticism and snark and judgment.

I wanted to wilt beneath you, become the paper that was crushed
up in your hand, my grey pulp snuggled warm within your
crevices. I wanted to be the gum on the ground as you trod
heavily with your peacock walk.

You tried to show that you didn't care when the truth was that
you cared too much.

I had never seen you so drunk before. You swayed and laughed
kept grabbing at my waist. You flailed around to the music and I
tried to keep up, disgusted by the old perverts drawn to you by
your baby face and sluttish ways.

They tried to drive me away and I gladly walked away, but you
kept finding me and pulling me back. The tiring circle of greed
and want made me weary, and the drink wasn't working on me, it
made me paranoid and insulted.

I felt claustrophobic inside the club, inside the smoke and the
neon's glow, and I felt trapped outside beneath the black sky and

the cigarettes. The box around us was tightening, the glass entrenched us like a cage, and the ice touch on my shoulders was heavy like the burden of pleasing you.

"I want to go home." I said.

You stopped in the middle of the road.

"I'll come with you." You said.
Were your eyes searching me or were they drifting in the cloud of alcohol?

"No, you stay here, stay out, and have fun." I nodded at the older gentlemen, your fans, sour in their history, cruel in their experience.

"I don't want to stay out."

"Why not?"

"Because I won't be with you."

I never knew it was possible to feel so elated and so pathetic at the same time. It was like bile and adrenaline poured through my veins in equal measure.

We walked to the bus stop, waved off the men standing outside the club. It was astounding to me, to see you shun such attention, to feel myself in the center of yours for the first time. I blossomed and died simultaneously, my bursts of colour washed over with the decaying rot of grey.

It was only ten minutes for the bus. We sat cross legged and you kissed me. It was spontaneous. I hadn't fought for it like I had had to do so much in the past for all your other kisses.
Your spit was still wet on my lips and right there for a minute I knew you so well.

I SWEAR THEY'RE OUT THERE

We drive and we drive and we drive. Through the nights we drive, through the rain and the thunderstorms. We stop at highway diners and stretch our money by sharing meals and drinking thick shakes to fill ourselves up. We stop at stores and buy apples and nuts to graze on, just so we can spend all our money on gas, just so we can keep on driving.

Dennis drives the most. He knows I hate it, and he knows he goes faster than I would ever dare to. So most of the time I sit with my seat wound back and my feet up on the dash. We play the radio loud and sing along, me more than him because even when it's just the two of us he feels silly when he sings. I don't care. I'm always singing.

In the back we have just our one bag, packed in a hurry when we made our last minute decision to just leave everything and go. I have the map on my lap but I never know how to read it or even know where we are, so we always have to pull over and Dennis studies it ruthlessly with his blue eyes and he always seems to know exactly where we are, or maybe he's guessing, and maybe he doesn't know.

But the roads keep coming, and we keep going. I keep my eyes on the skies, and I know Dennis wants to as well, but he has to keep his eyes ahead.

We sleep in the back. Our original plan was to take it in turns, but that changed when Dennis decided to do most of the driving, and also it got too lonely. So we stop in secluded areas and climb into the back seats which have been flattened down into the trunk, and we cover ourselves with blankets and have hot sweaty sex and then we fall asleep. We wake up cold under fogged up windows, and shiver as we put our clothes back on and Dennis groans as he climbs back behind the wheel, and he starts the car and lets everything warm up. Then we eat an apple or a handful of trail mix or whatever we have, and then we drive until we find a cheap place to drink coffee. Then our day begins again. We drive.

I know we're getting closer to where we're going because I can feel it. It's like a tingling sensation on my skin, like invisible webbing, like the feel you get when you touch a television screen. I know Dennis can feel it too, because he grips the steering wheel tighter.

I keep watching the skies.

One night we stop so Dennis can go piss behind a tree. I am alone in the car with the light on, and Dennis' door is slightly open. I can't see him outside in the black. I turn the radio up a little, but of all a sudden all it is it static. I try to turn the tuner but it all sounds the same, just white noise. Suddenly the car door swings open without a sound. I turn, expecting to see Dennis there, climbing into the car. But nobody is there. Just endless darkness outside.

Slowly I reach over, stretching out to try and close the door again, when it swings back towards me, slamming shut, plunging me into darkness. And I know then, by the prickly feeling on the back of my neck, that I'm not alone. I turn around quickly and see something move past my window. My heart feels like it stops for a second, and I crane my neck around to try and follow it, to see what it is, who it is, and where they're going.

But there's nothing there except the dark shade of the trees.

The car door opens again and the night outside vanishes as the light comes back on, and Dennis gets into the car. He looks at me, his hand on the key in the ignition. He knows something has happened.

"Something was here." Is all I say.

Things aren't the same after that. The radio comes back for a day but then is lost altogether to the static, and no amount of button turning will bring any listenable noise back. So we drive in silence.

When we sleep, we're constantly woken up by sounds outside. Tapping on the windows, or scratching on the paintwork. I'm a little afraid, and I tell Dennis this from behind my sunglasses one morning after spending a fitful night trying to sleep as the car shook softly from side to side. He comforts me by reminding me that this is what we came in search of. This is what we want.

"Do you realize how lucky we are? They made contact. They know where we're going."

And he's right. This is what we wanted. And every day he tells me we're getting closer to where we're headed.

And because we're getting closer, we don't bother with eating. We finish off the trail mix but then just spend our money which is almost all gone on gas and coffee. The nights become a blur of lights, and soon we don't even sleep, we just sit in the car, waiting.

When we get there, the place where everyone like us is headed, I'm a bit disappointed. It looks so ordinary. Like another field on another highway.

But at night things change. There are fantastic lights in the sky, the whole sky glowing as our friends show off, flying on and off our planet, into the black of space.

Dennis kisses me, and starts tearing at my clothes. I pull at his and soon we are both naked and running across the road and into the grass and mud. We run towards the lights which seem to get further from us the closer we get, like in a dream. Soon I feel violently sick, and my head pounds, but I keep running, feeling my feet sink into the mud, almost slipping, almost falling.

At one point I feel Dennis' hand slip from mine, but I don't stop, and when I look back I just see more lights and nothing else. I keep running, vomit gushing from my throat and out of my nose, and falling down in warm trickles across my neck and my breasts, but I don't stop.

I begin to scream as everything becomes too much to bear. And then the lights just vanish, and I am on my knees in the middle of the field, in the middle of the night. I don't know where Dennis is.

I catch my breath in the dark, and out of the corner of my eye I see on solitary light out in the distance. I begin to walk towards it, staggering almost. I get closer and closer, my chest burning, my throat sick and raw.

There's something different about this light. It doesn't seem to be drawing me like the others. It looks too simple, too plain.

I'm almost ten feet away when I see that it's a torch.

And I'm just five feet away when several black figures burst from behind it and pin me to the ground.

I begin to scream. I scream at them in spite of my scorched throat, in spite of the pounding in my chest. I scream that I saw them, that they were here, that they are, as Dennis and I have known all along, out there.

SEE HOW THEY GROW

I don't want to have sex with you, he says, and I certainly don't want to fall in love with you or see you as a person at all.

He stands up and takes off his clothes. His cock falls out of his pants, erect and ready.

He lies down on the bed next to me and I struggle out of my own trousers and look down at my own, feeling it between my fingers, limp and shy.

I just want to wank, he says, is that okay?

Well I have no choice, I think, what can I do? Throw you out of my house with no clothes on?

So I shrug, okay, yeah that's cool.

I begin trying to get hard, staring at his body, the trail of hair from his belly button down to his pubes, to the cock in his hand, pumping away, the foreskin sliding back and forth, down to his balls, then to his legs, and then down to his feet, crossed over each other at the ankle.

He has a soft sweet smell.

I spread my legs so that my knee touches his. He recoils, moving his leg away.

Then his hand comes down and envelopes my own hard cock, and begins to wank me off.

So I take his in my hand and feel myself mechanically begin to move up and down, up and down.

I'm hard but I feel nothing, I feel numb in my own groin. I stare out my window, feeling him next to me. I can tell his eyes are staring at my crotch.

I can feel his body tense as he gets close.

I keep pumping away with my own hand, not feeling anything under my palm, I am outside my body, floating somewhere near the ceiling, wishing I hadn't agreed to this, wondering how I had gotten so desperate.

He comes suddenly, without making any noise, hot spurts land across my arm and my shoulder, over my pillows.

I wilt under his hand.

I shrug and smile and say sometimes it just doesn't happen.

I'm a machine, I think, and I am malfunctioning this time.

MY BODY THE HAND GRENADE

My heart died when my cock died when it withered away because you took away your desire.

My last declaration of male a shriveled whimper of flesh, lying between skinny thighs, under narrow hips and my ribs.

You told me you would never touch me again and my body desiccated, inside behind my bony cage my heart shook and turned into a sour patch, lodged between my lungs.

I stood in the morning air and took in the sweetness of the first light but it didn't help at all. My heart died and it went away, and I crawled back into my bed, alone, and felt nothing beat through my chest, through my veins, everything lay flat.

There was no reason for me to rise anymore, no reason for my heart to pump, for want and need and crave to flood between my legs, to make my skin thistle and raise in tiny bumps.

No shiver down my spine, no chill on the back of my neck. Inside of me dirty water pumped, my ugly corpse the dam which held everything back.

With my eyes closed I wished it would turn into gasoline, into a flammable dangerous fluid, coursing through my veins.

And with your rejection, like a tiny spark, I'd ignite, and my hideous shell would burst, I'd incinerate, and in a beautiful burst of light I would vanish, forever.

SADNESS OF LOVE

We hung out at the pier, in the sun we dipped our feet into the water and watched the sun sprinkle diamonds across the top of the sea.

He wore cut off dungarees and sunglasses, and we touched toes under the water.

It had been a quick summer. The April showers had outstayed their welcome and hung around until mid-June. Then the sun scorched and blazed and all our free time was eaten up by work and hungover days and Junior's funeral.

We hung out at the rock bar most nights, the sweltering heat making everyone melt. We'd walk home at sunrise, drink beer in the garden and fall asleep on blankets, or on deckchairs. We'd light candles to keep the mosquitoes away and sit in the glow eating barbeque food. We'd fuck wildly on the kitchen floor at three in the morning, and lie panting in a daze of drunkenness and ecstasy.

But it had been so quick.

All this had happened in a flash of memory behind my eyes.

It was the last real day of summer. Before he had to go away. We had walked to the pier and had drunk wine and gone to sit by the water. It was meant to be the perfect end. Some fitting finale to a season of memories. But we had barely spoken the past few days.

I had tried to touch him but he had recoiled under the covers, and the night before he had refused to come to bed at all. The chasm between us yawned, even as we played footsie under the water.

And as the sun went down and the water cooled, he stretched and took his foot away, pulling his knees up to hug them. The chill set in the air and he got up and left.

I didn't follow him. Instead I kept my feet in the water, and felt the water grow colder and colder until I sat shivering in the dark.

I had asked him on the train to the pier what had happened between us.

He said the slow fade of love.

GRINDR LOVE STORY

There's a pecking order to this I think, as I skim through the
rules: NO FEMS, NO CAMP, NO WEIRDOS, NO TIME
WASTERS.
The grinning faces leer out at me, filtered and altered and warped
beyond recognition. Guys who are looking for friendship, or
dates, or something serious; definitely NOT NSA, or "fun", or "a
quick shag", because if that's what you're looking for you can
LEAVE NOW.
The same guys who then pose in their underwear, bulging
crotches displayed between their spread legs, stomachs sucked in,
lips pouting.
Just a casual look, I think, casual and typical, nothing sexual
here.

STR8-ACTING screams some guy, as he poses, neck bent,
showing off the stars tattooed from behind his ear down his neck,
in the gym mirror, before going on to describe things he enjoys,
things like RIMMING and COTTAGING and ANAL and ORAL
and THREESOMES and VERBAL/GOB. He is also interested in
meeting types like TWINKS and BUILDERS and GEEKS and
MARRIED MEN.

There are SORTED, NO DRAMA, DECENT men who will meet
you in the dark, high and begging to be sucked, their limp dicks

"rock solid on the way here". Never 100% gay, always open minded, "just trying it out".

"Just seeing what's out there" might mean "let's fuck for the weekend then I'll forget you exist", or even "let's cybersex every night and then I'll vanish".

The boyfriend hunters will attack you with hundreds of questions, soaking up information like dying sponges lost out of the oceans, wanting to get to know you, wanting to be able to lick the inside of you before they even meet you, anything to change that dreaded SINGLE status to IN A RELATIONSHIP. Like truffle hogs in the mud they scuffle and snort as they try to decide if you're worth the shag, worth introducing to their mates, able to prove your worth if they deign to grace you with the title of BOYFRIEND.

This dystopian nightmare is all at my fingertips; like crack in bleak lonely evenings, like poisonous gas when I feel empty and shit.

It's all here, thousands of pictures, hundreds of promises, millions of rules, READ THE PROFILE - if you're old you've had it, PERVERT.

Lust strikes like static shocks, love trickles through, like grey lumpless vomit, cooling quickly, pooling in the cracks, and I try to make sense of it.

SPACE MAN

You come to me in a dream. Like the sun walking through the door. A neon sun you hurt my eyes with your purity.
Your beauty radiates in colours that don't exist.
You lie next to me on the bed. We fuck. A man walks into the room, confused, it's suddenly dark. When he leaves you're suddenly dressed, and you keep kissing me and somehow I know there's somebody else, somebody you love very much, somebody who understands you, all the way deep down into your core.
My own core rattles me awake, and I lie in the dark, thinking about you and your shining, you the person who doesn't exist, who came bubbling out of the electric pulses in my sleeping brain, a spark, a tiny malfunction, manifested by the black pit lodged somewhere behind my ribs.
The rain pours down and inside my head you are as far away as you can ever possibly be.

GIVE ME YOUR EYES

Laid out on my bed he's already taken off his shirt and is unbuttoning his jeans. I shut the door behind me and turn off the light, leaving the room in the multicolour dazzle of the fairy lights which coil around the bars of the headboard. I sit on the bed beside him and he pulls of his jeans in one swift motion and his arms coil around me, his heavy breath on my neck, the stubble of chin scraping my cheek, the rustle of hair in my ear. I shiver as he pulls off my shirt and his fingers go to work on my zipper. I drag my fingers down his back, manoeuvring beneath him. He lies down on top of me, hot wet mouth searching out mine, noses grazing together, I push my tongue inside behind his teeth, he bites my bottom lip. I wrap my legs around him, my heel digging into the back of his thigh the back of his knees. He pulls my arms up over my head, licks my neck, bites me. We roll over, as he pulls me up on top of him. I cup his face as I lean down and kiss him, hard, licking at the sides of his mouth, under his nose, kissing the lids of his eyes, inhaling his scent from his hair. He grips my hips and a rhythm breaks out, narrated by the click of the bed beneath us. His eyes flutter open, in the kaleidoscope of pleasure and lights I see him stare up at me, a smile curls at the corners of his mouth.

"You're gorgeous"

He keeps looking at me. Then he closes his eyes. I have my palms pressed against his chest. I move them up to his face as I contemplate what he's just said. He kisses my hands gently.

I am confused by his words. Unable to correlate the fact that he was looking at me while he said them. He opens his eyes again. The smile returns. He pushes his head back and groans. I try to imagine what he sees. My own body curled up, sitting astride him, lit up by the garish fairy lights, some sins hidden in shadows, but the worst attributes still there, my face and my features.

I can't imagine what else he must see. But a fire inside begins to burn, and I realise I have to find out.

It seems simple, such a simple answer. I am still touching his face, so I move my fingers up over his eyelids. I begin to move my hips faster, and he starts to groan again. Quickly I pull up his eyelids and dig my fingers in. I feel the whisper of his eyelashes on my fingertips for less than half a second, and then I feel the eyes themselves, soft but firm, like peeled grapes.

I dig my fingers in further, feeling warm mush as he begins to shake beneath me. His groan turns into a whine and then a strangled scream as blood begins to run down the back of his throat. I pull at the eyes, trying to keep them in my grasp. I feel tiny threads tear and rip as I yank them out of their caves.

For a second, beneath me, I see his screaming face, the big bloody holes, the big bloody tears pouring down over my pillow. But I've got them, his eyes, and now I can see.

THIS IS WHY I GET DRUNK

the first guy I ever made it
with was an arrogant
mommy's boy who
had once weighed sixteen stone
and still seemed bitter
that he hadn't been born as
perfect as he now thought he was.

after kissing in a nightclub
we met up again and
he saw me in the cold light
of the day and
lied to my face and I believed
him and a week later
he had a new boyfriend.

the first guy I ever
slept with was a man I had
never seen before and he flirted
with me in the urinal
of a nightclub. He laughed
at my red trousers and I laughed
at him.

he took me home and fucked me
and it really hurt and he begged
me to swallow his cum so i
tried but it was harsh and bitter
and I spat it out over his stomach.

he drove me home
the next morning in a really old
car and I lay on the sofa hungover
and hurting and
didn't feel any different.

I didn't see him again until a year
later and I was dancing on
the stage of the nightclub with my friends,
I had a beer in my hand, I felt good,
and I looked up, he mouthed the word
"disgusting" at me across the floor,
so I smiled at him.

the first guy who I
thought broke my heart had
tattoos up and down his arms.
I knew by now that boys would
say anything to get as far as
possible as quickly as possible so

they could see if you were worth
bothering with.

it was over Christmas and we spoke
every day and he was funny and
different and he took me out
to dinner and kissed me and let
me suck his tiny cock and it tasted
of nothing. he was so inoffensive.

but he began to grow colder
by the minute and one morning
he wouldn't let me touch him
and we walked into town,
he took a shortcut
through the park and left me
by the graveyard
in the wintery
cold sun, and that night
he told me he didn't want to
see me again.

the first guy to ruin everything
was young but wise
beyond his years and we would
meet up in the

early hours
of the morning and fuck
and I liked that I knew nothing
much about him.

but he wanted to be friends
and invited me to gatherings
and parties
and nightclubs.
I felt wildly contradicted
and helplessly lost
if we did not have sex
each time that we met up.

the more time we spent
together, the wider my
scope into his life became
and I'd know that he'd
fucked other people that i
knew, or had fucked, and
the wires crossed far too
messily for me.
it became harder
not to care. I felt myself
losing control of it all. I hated him
at times just like I hated myself.

and when I lay in the bed as he

fucked somebody else next to me,

I knew that things had gone

terribly wrong, and yet

it felt perfectly right

at the same time.

it was keeping in with the theme,

the pattern I had

grown to see.